FOOD CHAINS

MEADOW FOOD CHAINS

Bobbie Kalman and Kelley MacAulay

A Crabtree Crown Book

Crabtree Publishing
crabtreebooks.com

MEADOW FOOD CHAINS

Created by Bobbie Kalman

Editor-in-chief
Bobbie Kalman

Writing team
Bobbie Kalman
Kelley MacAulay

Substantive editor
Kathryn Smithyman

Editors
Molly Aloian
Kristina Lundblad

Production manager
Candice Campbell

Design
Margaret Salter

Consultant
Patricia Loesche, Ph.D., Animal Behavior Program, Department of Psychology, University of Washington

Cover
Rhea Magaro-Wallace

Images
All images: Shutterstock.com

Crabtree Publishing

crabtreebooks.com 800-387-7650

In Canada: We acknowledge the financial support of the Government of Canada through the Canada Book Fund for our publishing activities.

Printed in the U.S.A./CP032026

Published in Canada
Crabtree Publishing
616 Welland Ave.
St. Catharines, Ontario
L2M 5V6

Published in the United States
Crabtree Publishing
347 Fifth Ave.
Suite 1402-145
New York, NY 10016

Library and Archives Canada Cataloguing in Publication
Available at the Library and Archives Canada

Library of Congress Cataloging-in-Publication Data
Available at the Library of Congress

Hardcover: 978-1-0398-7296-7
Paperback: 978-1-0398-7354-4
Ebook (pdf): 978-1-0398-7405-3
Epub: 978-1-0398-7454-1

CONTENTS

WHAT IS A MEADOW?

A meadow is an **undisturbed area** where different types of grasses and flowers grow. Meadows are open places with few trees. They often receive a lot of sunshine and can be hot places in summer. The soil becomes dry when meadows do not receive much rain. There are many kinds of animals that live in or around meadows. Some of these animals are large, and others are small.

Wide open spaces

Meadows are a lot like **grasslands**. Grasslands are areas where grasses and some flowers grow. Many animals, such as the bison below, live in grasslands. Grasslands are much larger areas than are meadows. Meadows and grasslands often grow in different places. Grasslands do not grow near oceans, but meadows can grow anywhere!

Where are meadows?

Meadows grow in many places. Some grow on the edges of **wetlands**. Wetlands are areas of land that are wet for at least part of the year. Meadows on the edges of wetlands are called **wet meadows**.

Other meadows grow in forest **clearings**, or areas where no trees grow. Some meadows, such as the one shown below, grow on the edges of forests. This book is about meadows that grow on the edges of forests.

WHAT IS A FOOD CHAIN?

There are many plants and animals on Earth! Plants and animals are living things. Living things need air, water, sunlight, and food to stay alive.

Staying alive

Plants and animals get **nutrients** from food. Nutrients are substances that plants and animals need to grow and to stay healthy. Animals also get **energy** from food. Animals use energy to breathe air, to grow, and to move around.

This butterfly is getting nutrients and energy from a flower.

Producing food

Plants **produce**, or make, their own food! They make food by catching some of the sun's energy and changing it into the nutrients they need. Plants are the only living things that make their own food.

Eating food

Animals must eat food to get nutrients. Some animals eat plants. Others eat animals that have fed on plants. This pattern of eating and being eaten is called a **food chain**. All plants and animals are part of food chains.

Energy from the sun

Green plants use energy from the sun to make food. They use some of the food energy and store the rest.

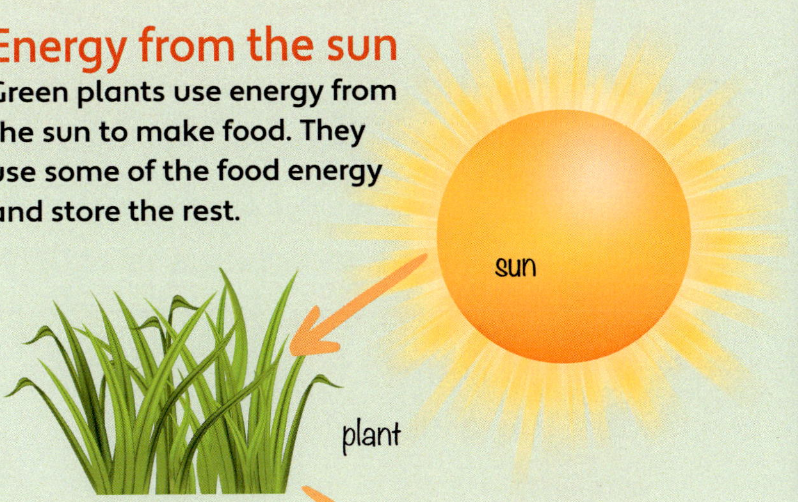

When an animal such as a squirrel eats a plant, it gets some of the energy that was stored in the plant. The squirrel gets less of the sun's energy than the plant received.

When a fox eats a squirrel, energy is passed to the fox through the squirrel. The fox gets less of the sun's energy than the amount the squirrel received.

AN ENERGY PYRAMID

When animals eat other living things, their bodies take in energy. The pattern created as energy travels along food chains is called an **energy pyramid**. The first level of the pyramid is wide to show that there are many plants. The second level narrows to show that there are fewer animals than there are plants. The top level contains even fewer animals. Find out why on page 9!

Third level: carnivores

The third level of a food chain is made up of **carnivores.** Carnivores are animals that get energy by eating other animals. Carnivores are the **secondary consumers** in a food chain.

Secondary consumers eat primary consumers. Secondary consumers are at the top of the food chain, where there is much less energy. For this reason, there are fewer carnivores than there are herbivores or plants.

Second level: herbivores

The second level of a food chain is made up of **herbivores.** Herbivores are animals that eat mainly plants. Herbivores are the **primary consumers** in a food chain.

Primary consumers are the first living things in a food chain that must eat to get energy. Herbivores must eat many plants to get the energy they need to survive. For this reason, there are fewer herbivores than there are plants.

First level: plants

The **primary**, or first, level of a food chain is made up of plants. Plants are called **primary producers** because they make food and are the first link in a food chain. There are more plants than there are animals. It takes many plants to feed all the animals in a food chain!

HOW PLANTS MAKE FOOD

Plants use sunlight to make food. This process is called **photosynthesis**. Plants contain a green **pigment**, or natural color, in their leaves called **chlorophyll**. Chlorophyll has two jobs. First, it catches sunlight.

Next, chlorophyll combines the sunlight with water and **carbon dioxide** to make the plant's food. Water is in the soil, and carbon dioxide is a gas found in air. The food a plant makes is called **glucose**. Glucose is a type of sugar.

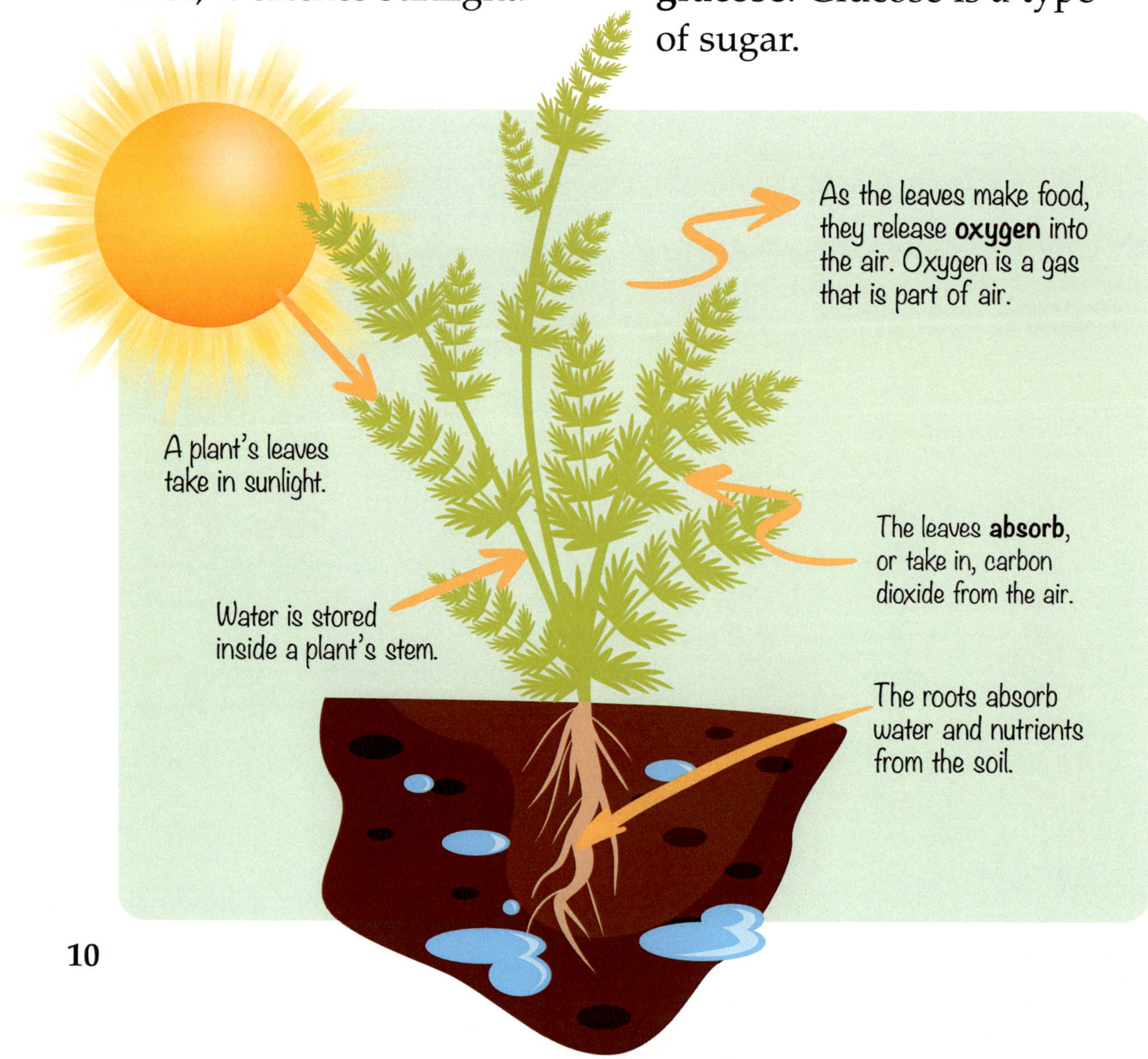

Clean air

Plants help keep animals alive. As plants make food, they also make large amounts of oxygen. Animals must breathe oxygen to survive. Plants help animals by releasing oxygen, but they also help animals by removing some carbon dioxide from the air. Too much carbon dioxide in the air is harmful to animals.

MEADOW PLANTS

Meadows are filled with many types of tall grasses, **shrubs**, and colorful flowers. Except in wet meadows, the soil in most meadows is **sandy loam**. Sandy loam is a dry soil that has few of the nutrients needed by plants.

Daisies are flowers that grow well in the loose, sandy soil found in meadows.

Changing to survive

Plants that grow in meadows have **adapted**, or changed to survive. Most meadows are home to many types of wildflowers. Wildflowers have long roots. Long roots help these plants survive during **droughts**. Droughts are dry periods when very little rain falls. When the ground is dry, the long roots of wildflowers are able to reach water deep within the soil.

Stay out!

The grasses that grow in meadows have roots that grow tightly together. Tight roots leave little room for other plants to grow. With fewer plants growing in meadows, there is more water for the grasses.

HERBIVORES ARE PLANT-EATERS

Cottontail rabbits are grazers. They eat mainly grasses.

Deer are browsers. They eat mainly leaves and twigs.

Many kinds of animals live in meadows. Forest animals also look for food in meadows. Some of the animals that feed in meadows are herbivores. Herbivores use a lot of energy searching for plants to eat. They have to eat many plants to get the food energy they need.

Herbivore food

Different herbivores eat different types of plants. Herbivores that eat grasses and small plants near the ground are called **grazers**. Those that eat the leaves, twigs, and shoots of plants are known as **browsers**.

Eating different parts

Some herbivores eat many plant parts, including flowers, fruits, nuts, and seeds. Other herbivores eat only one part of plants, such as **nectar**. Nectar is a sweet liquid found in flowers. Hummingbirds have long, thin beaks that reach the nectar found deep inside flowers.

MEADOW ANIMALS

Meadows are full of living things. The different plants that grow in them attract many kinds of animals. Some of the animals eat the plants, and some make homes among the tall grasses. Meadow animals have many ways of surviving in the wide open spaces where they live. For example, the fur of a snowshoe hare is brown in the summer but changes to white in the winter. By changing color, the snowshoe hare can blend in with the land both in summer and winter. These pages show some of the other ways animals survive in meadows.

Chipmunks eat fruits and seeds, but these foods are hard to find in winter. Chipmunks have special pouches in their cheeks that can hold food. They use the pouches to gather as much food as they can. They then hide the food and find more to store. During winter, chipmunks eat the stored food so they will not go hungry.

Living underground

Many meadow animals, such as marmots, protect themselves by living in underground homes called **burrows.** Most burrows have several rooms where the animals sleep and store food. If an animal is startled while it is gathering food above ground, it can run into its burrow.

Hunting at night

Wide open meadows may look completely empty during the day. They seem empty because many meadow animals, such as this badger, are **nocturnal**. Nocturnal animals become active at **dusk**, or in the evening, and hunt during the night. They sleep in their safe burrows during the day.

CARNIVORES IN A MEADOW

Meadows are home to many carnivores. Most carnivores are **predators**, or animals that hunt and kill other animals for food. The animals that predators eat are called **prey**. Predators that eat herbivores are called secondary consumers.

Tertiary consumers

Some predators do not eat just herbivores. They also eat other carnivores. When carnivores eat other carnivores, they are called **tertiary consumers**.

Two different meals

The golden eagle, shown above, is a secondary consumer when it eats a herbivore such as a rabbit. When it eats a young fox, which is a carnivore, the eagle is a tertiary consumer.

Hunting the weak

Carnivores help keep meadow animal **populations** healthy by feeding on the weakest animals. The weakest animals are usually the very young, sick, or old animals. Carnivores hunt these animals because they are easy to catch. By hunting the weak animals, carnivores remove them from food chains. Without these animals, there is more food for healthy meadow animals.

Pest control!

Some herbivores, such as mice, rats, and rabbits, have many babies. These animals are said to be **pests** because they strip bark off trees, move into people's yards and homes, and carry diseases. Predators help keep the populations of pest animals under control.

Bobcats are meadow predators that hunt many small animals. By eating these animals, bobcats help make sure that there will not be too many meadow herbivores.

FINDING FOOD

Predators have many ways of catching food in a meadow. Some predators, such as the praying mantis shown right, sit and wait for their prey in plain sight! The praying mantis is difficult to see because its body has **camouflage**, or coloring that blends in with its surroundings. The insect is so well hidden that, when prey is nearby, it can simply reach out and grab the prey!

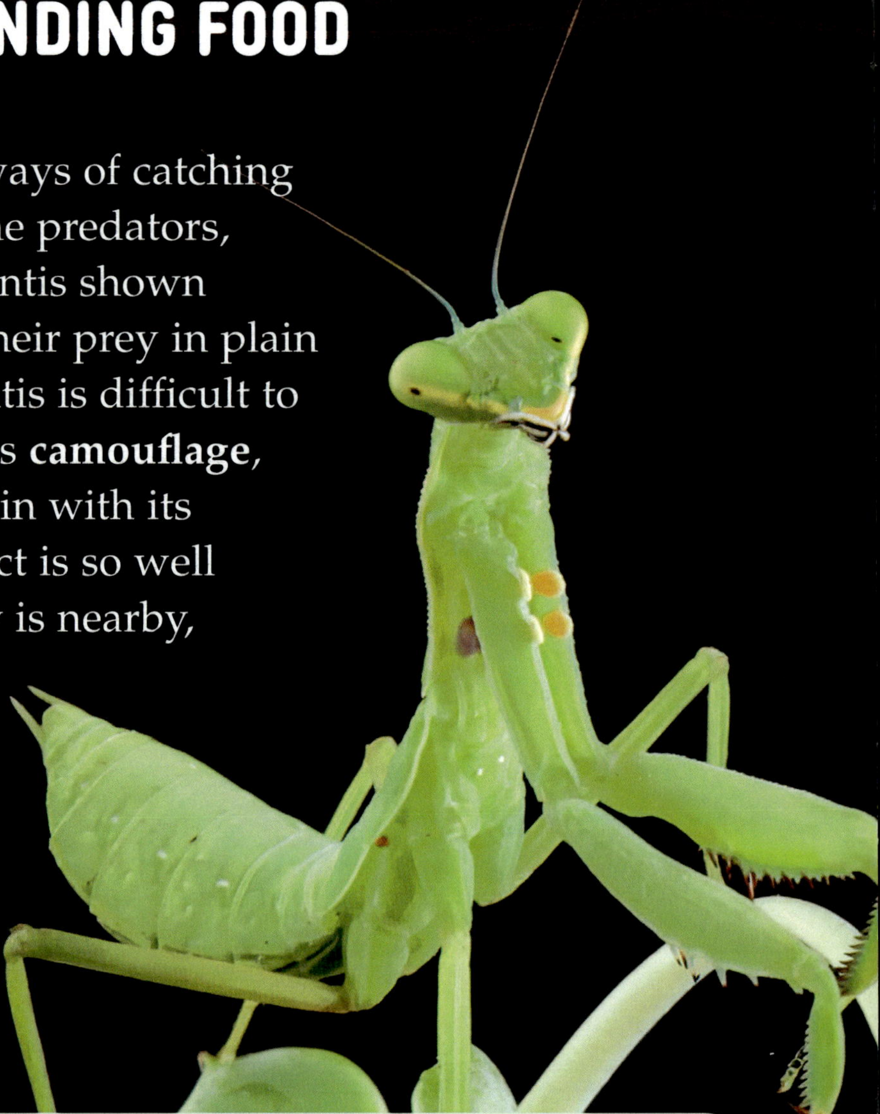

Capturing prey

Most predators also have senses and body parts that help them catch prey. For example, barn owls, shown right, have very good eyesight and hearing. When the owls fly above meadows, they can see and hear prey far below them on the ground. Barn owls use their sharp **talons**, or claws, to catch the prey.

Eating the leftovers

Some carnivores do not hunt. Instead, they feed mainly on **carrion**, or dead animals. Carnivores that feed on carrion are called **scavengers**. If an animal is killed by a predator, the scavengers must wait until the predator has finished eating. The scavengers can then move in and feed on the leftovers.

Removing the waste

Scavengers keep meadows clean by eating carrion. If they did not eat carrion, meadows would soon be filled with dead bodies! Scavengers use the leftover food energy in carrion and keep it from going to waste.

MEADOW OMNIVORES

Some meadow animals eat both plants and animals. They are called **omnivores**. Skunks, such as the one shown below, are omnivores that live in meadows. They eat mice and insects, as well as berries and other plant foods. Omnivores belong to several levels of a food chain, depending on the kinds of foods they eat.

Opportunistic feeders

Omnivores are **opportunistic feeders**, or animals that eat almost any food that is available. Opportunistic feeders do not have much difficulty finding a meal because they eat any food they can find!

Different diets

An omnivore's **diet**, or the types of foods it eats, often changes with the seasons. Many omnivores eat animals and insects for part of the year and plant foods at other times. For example, red foxes, shown below, eat mainly rabbits and other small animals in summer. In winter, when prey animals are harder to find, red foxes also eat plant foods.

Perfect omnivores

Foxes eat almost anything they can swallow! They can survive anywhere, but meadows provide them with many kinds of foods. When there are no animals to hunt, foxes can live on fruits. As predators, foxes kill small prey such as mice, rats, and voles. A fox **pounces**, or leaps quickly, on an animal in the same way a cat pounces on a mouse! By pouncing, foxes can surprise their prey. Their footsteps do not give them away. Like cats, foxes also like to play with their food before eating it.

MEADOW DECOMPOSERS

Scavengers eat dead things, but they often leave bones and other animal parts behind. **Decomposers** are living things that finish the job! They eat the leftover parts of dead plants and animals. Termites, worms, and snails are some common decomposers found in meadows.

What is detritus?

Decomposers make up **detritus food chains**. Detritus is material that is **decomposing**, or breaking down.

A detritus food chain

When a plant or an animal, such as this bird, dies, it becomes dead material in the soil. Its body contains some energy even after it is dead.

Decomposers living in the soil, such as this snail, eat the dead material. As they eat, the decomposers get some of the stored energy. They then pass some of this energy into the soil through their droppings.

The stored energy in the droppings of decomposers adds nutrients to the soil. The nutrients help plants grow.

Note: The arrows point toward the living things that receive energy.

Nutrients in the soil

Decomposers such as earthworms help keep the soil healthy for plants. When they eat dead plants and animals, they use the energy that is left over in them. They then put some of this energy back into the soil through their droppings. Earthworms also add air to the soil when they dig tunnels. Water reaches the roots of plants more easily through these tunnels. The water carries nutrients to the plants.

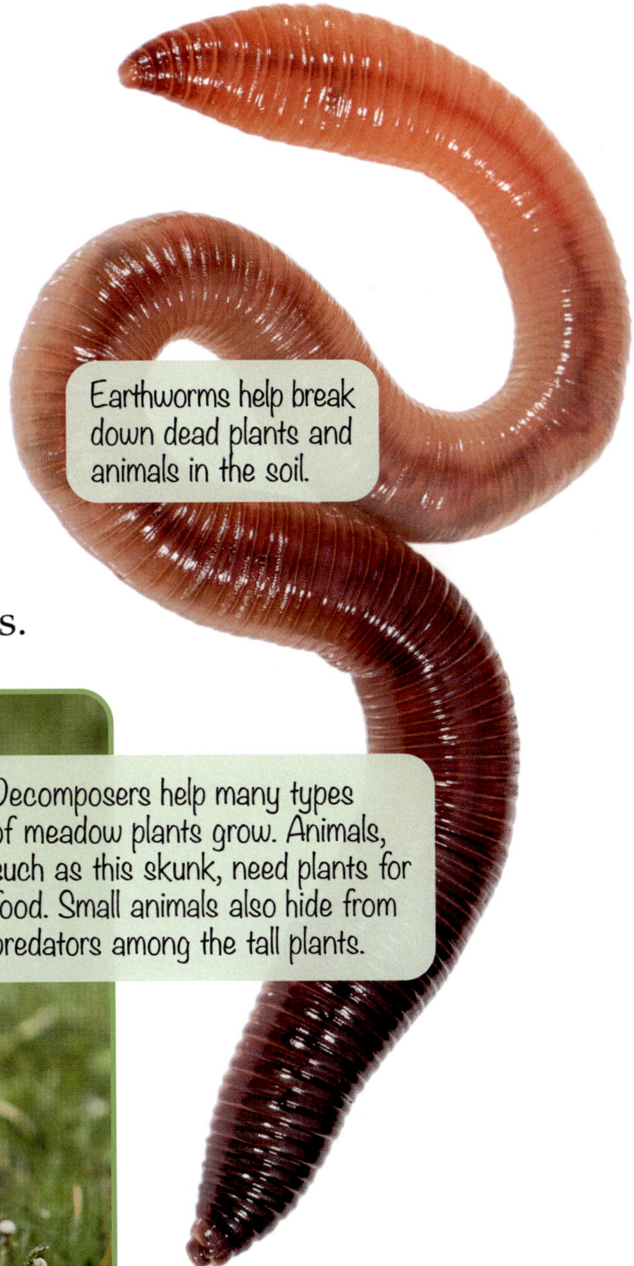

Earthworms help break down dead plants and animals in the soil.

Decomposers help many types of meadow plants grow. Animals, such as this skunk, need plants for food. Small animals also hide from predators among the tall plants.

A MEADOW FOOD WEB

Most plants and animals belong to many food chains. A single food chain includes a plant, a herbivore, and a carnivore. When an animal from one food chain eats a plant or an animal that belongs to a different food chain, two food chains connect. When two or more food chains connect, a **food web** is formed. There are many food webs in a meadow.

A summer food web

This diagram shows a meadow food web during summer. The arrows point toward the living things that receive the food energy.

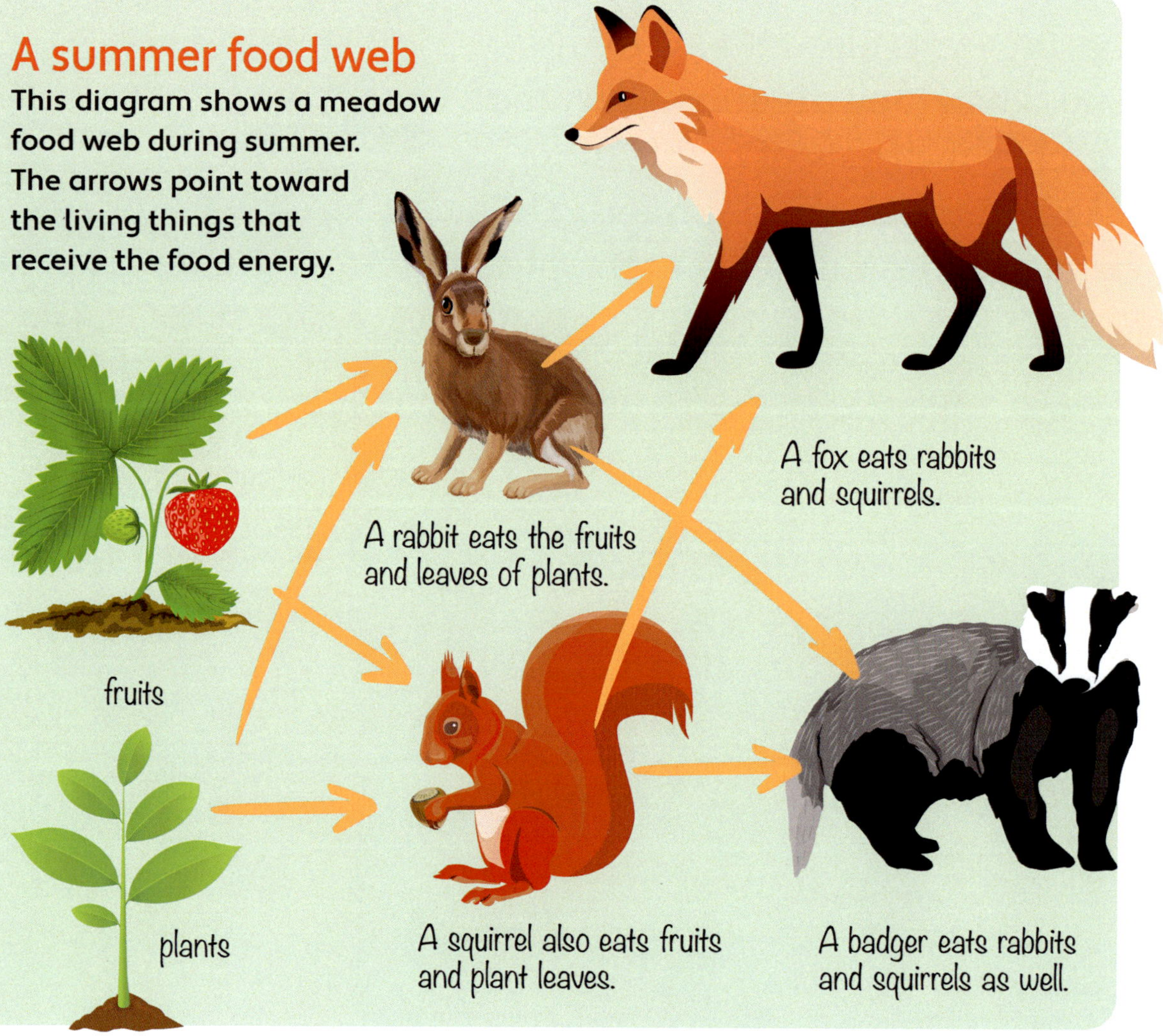

Moving with the seasons

Meadow food webs change with the seasons. Some animals, such as monarch butterflies, cannot survive in cold weather. They **migrate**, or travel long distances to warmer places. In autumn, monarchs migrate to California and Mexico, where the weather is warm all year. When the butterflies arrive, they change the food webs in California and Mexico. For example, black-eared mice feed on monarchs while the butterflies are in Mexico. When the butterflies leave, black-eared mice find other foods to eat.

DANGERS TO MEADOW FOOD WEBS

Meadows are important places for many types of plants and animals, but people are changing them. They are moving into meadow land in large numbers. They use the space to build cities, farms, and golf courses.

Before they build, people clear, or remove the plants from, meadows. Some of the animals that lived among the grasses and flowers are forced to move to other areas. Many meadow animals die, however, when their food and homes are gone.

People have cleared thousands of acres of meadow land to plant crops or to provide space for cows and other animals to graze. As the animals graze, they eat many of the plants that meadow animals need for food.

Moving into meadows

When people clear the plants from a meadow, they remove one link of a food chain. When a link in a food chain is gone, all the other links in the food chain suffer.

Losing their food

Without plants to eat, many herbivores die from **starvation**. When the herbivores are gone, carnivores, such as this coyote, have no food. Before long, many carnivores also starve.

HELPING MEADOWS

Meadow animals need meadow plants to survive. As meadows are destroyed, many meadow animals are left without food to eat and places to live. To help meadow animals, many people grow meadows in their back yards.

Ask your parents if your family can plant a meadow. Be sure to plant **native plants**! Native plants are plants that grow naturally in an area. By planting native plants, you will give many birds, insects, and small animals places to live.

Monarchs and milkweed

Before planting your meadow, find out which native plants will help the animals living in your area. For example, if you want to attract monarch butterflies to your meadow, you must plant milkweed. Monarch butterflies cannot survive without these plants because the butterflies lay their eggs only on milkweed. Monarch babies hatch from the eggs as caterpillars, which feed on the milkweed plants. By planting milkweed, your meadow will provide a home for many monarch butterflies.

Keep out of my space!

Many people enjoy visiting meadows, but meadows are damaged when people ride bicycles and motorcycles through them. The tires damage many types of plants. If people keep riding over the same areas, the plants never grow back. Animals need these plants for food. Motorcycles and other off-road vehicles are also very noisy. Animals, such as the squirrel shown right, are scared of the noise and have to find new places to live.

Keeping meadows safe

Scientists study meadows and the plants and animals that live there. Studying meadows helps them find out how meadows are being damaged. There are many things you can do to keep meadows safe for animals. Remember that these areas need to be undisturbed. Always walk around a meadow instead of through it. Never ride your bicycle in a meadow.

Having a meadow in your back yard will help you enjoy and learn about many plants and animals.

GLOSSARY

Note: Boldfaced words that are defined in the text may not appear in the glossary.

carbon dioxide A gas found in air that is needed by plants to make food

energy The power living things get from food that helps them move, grow, and stay healthy

oxygen A colorless, odorless gas in air that animals need to breathe

pest An animal considered troublesome to humans

pigment A natural color found in plants and animals

population The total number of one type of plant or animal living in a certain place

shrub A plant that grows low to the ground and has many stems; a bush

starvation Suffering that results from a lack of food

undisturbed area An area of land that has not been changed by people

INDEX